DON'T FORGET YOUR BREAKFAST

A 5 MINUTE DAILY DEVOTIONAL

BY
TAMI WILLIAMS

Don't Forget Your Breakfast by Tami Williams

Copyright © 2019 by Tami Williams

1588 Fitzgerald Drive #262 Pinole, CA 94564

Book cover design: Andrés Matute

INTRODUCTION

I wrote this devotional because the initial idea of setting aside 20 minutes every morning seemed overwhelming. I was busy. I couldn't wrap my head around getting up earlier. I was already tired, and I felt maxed out! Yet, I wanted more than simply church on Sunday mornings or saying I loved God.

In Proverbs 4:20-21 it says, "My child, pay attention to what I say. Listen carefully to my words. Don't lose sight of them. Let them penetrate deep into your heart." Then, Proverbs 4:23 brings it home by stating, "Guard your heart above all else, for it determines the course of our life." Hmmm, well, the quality of my life is at stake, and it was going to be kind of hard to write God's word deep in my heart without putting forth some effort to consistently read his word and hear his voice.

So, I had 2 choices. I could keep doing what I was doing knowing nothing would change. OR, I could start somewhere. I decided to start with a few minutes while I had breakfast (aka coffee and a snack). I had nothing to lose, so it certainly wasn't going to hurt.

This is an invitation to have a daily bite of God's word. *I believe that this next month will create a divine appetite inside of you for more of God.*

DAY 1

"You crown the year with a bountiful harvest; even the hard pathways overflow with abundance." - Psalms 65:11

Hello, there. Real quick, close your eyes and imagine a picture of the best dad in the whole world smiling at his kid. Seriously, do it. Do you have a visual? That is God right now!! He is so happy that you are committing 5 minutes at the start of your day to him.

It doesn't matter what month or day you are starting this devotional. God cares about your year. He cares about you.

Prayer: Lord, I pray that you would instill a hope in me for the year ahead and the harvest you have for me. Help me to be consistent over the next few weeks in my prayer time.

Today's Proclamation: **Today is a new day. I'm looking forward, not backward.**

"SAMUEL DID NOT YET KNOW THE LORD BECAUSE HE HAD NEVER HAD A MESSAGE FROM THE LORD BEFORE."

1 Samuel 3:7

Day 2

*To walk on God's path for your life,
you must hear his voice.*

Do you know God's voice? Do you listen when he provides instruction? Did you know that even during one point in his life, mighty Samuel didn't know the Lord's voice (1 Samuel 3:7)? If Samuel can learn to recognize God's voice, then so can you.

Prayer: Lord, I pray that you would speak, and I would hear your voice. I would hear it clearly without a doubt. I would not only hear; I would also have faith in your instructions.

Today's Proclamation: **Speak, Lord, for your servant hears!**

DAY 3

*1 Peter 4:10 – "God has given you a gift
from his great variety of spiritual gifts.
Use them well to serve one another."*

The key here is to use the gifts. Your relationships can flourish when you learn how to show God's love and help others through the use of your gifts. Do you know what your gifts are? Are you using them to the fullest?

Prayer: Lord, show me the gifts you've given me and how to use them to show love to others. I am thanking you in advance for showing me. I am grateful for the gifts you have given me. Give me a desire to use my gifts more and more every day.

Today's Proclamation: **I have a great gift from God.**

DAY 4

Luke 1:37 – "For the word of God will never fail."

Sometimes when God is speaking to us about our gifts or instructions about a situation, we doubt the likelihood of what we are hearing. You might even think to yourself, "There's no way!" Well, his word says that with God nothing is impossible. When God tells you, listen to his instructions.

Prayer: Lord, I am opening my ears to hear your instructions. As I hear your voice, let it be done in my life according to your word. I pray for confirmation of your instructions. Thank you for reassuring me.

Today's Proclamation: **Regardless of the circumstance, nothing is impossible to God.**

DAY 5

Psalms 6:8-9 – "Go away, all you who do evil, for the Lord has heard my weeping. The Lord has heard my plea; the Lord will answer my prayer."

There is an abundance of grace and mercy at the cross. He doesn't get embarrassed, and you shouldn't either. It's also not about making you feel bad. The fact is that God already knows every single detail. You might as well talk to him about what is going on in your life and ask for guidance. He listens and hears your prayers.

Prayer: Lord, thank you for hearing me when I cry out to you. Sometimes I hold back talking to you about what's going on even when I shouldn't. Help me to release any feelings or thoughts that would try to keep me from talking to you. I ask for your divine grace and mercy in my life.

Today's Proclamation: **God hears me when I pray.**

"IF YOU ARE FILLED
WITH LIGHT, WITH NO
DARK CORNERS, THEN
YOUR WHOLE LIFE WILL
BE RADIANT, AS
THOUGH A FLOODLIGHT
WERE FILLING YOU
WITH LIGHT."

Luke 11:36

DAY 6

"For the word of God is alive and powerful. It is sharper than the sharpest two-edged sword, cutting between soul and spirit, between joint and marrow. It exposes our innermost thoughts and desires."

- Hebrews 4:12

Yikes, he knows all that! At first, it can seem scary that God knows your deepest secrets. Then again, since he knows you are free to open up to him. His word can be a lamp to your life. Let God's light shine on every area of your life (Luke 11:36). There is no reason to hide any aspect of your life from God. He knows, and He loves you.

Prayer: Lord, you know the areas of my life that are dim. Align my thoughts and desires to your word. Bring your light to every corner.

Today's Proclamation: **There will be light where there is darkness, and I will let my light shine.**

DAY 1

It's a humble act to ask God for help. He wants us to be humble, so he can lift us up (Luke 14:11). God doesn't need you to tell him what is going on; he wants a relationship with you. He wants a two-way conversation. After you pray, spend a couple of minutes waiting for God's response.

Prayer: Lord, please guide and direct me in all areas of my life. Teach me how to build a stronger relationship with you. Thank you for waking me up this morning. Thank you for your divine direction. I pray that you would speak to me.

Today's Proclamation: I don't have all the answers, but God does, and that's what matters.

"Don't worry about anything; instead, pray about everything. Tell God what you need, and thank him for all he has done. Then, you will experience God's peace, which exceeds anything we can understand. His peace will guard your hearts and minds as you live in Christ Jesus."

Philippians 4:6-7

DAY 8

Giving *thanks* ahead of time is a form of faith and anticipation. Jesus gave thanks first (John 11:41). When you prayerfully bring your requests to God with thanksgiving in your heart, you don't have to be anxious (Philippians 4:6).

Prayer: Lord, I am thankful for the work that you are doing that I can't see. You know all the details and exactly what I need, even better than I do. I thank you for bringing the help, guidance, and tools that I need.

Today's Proclamation: **I am thankful that God hears my requests and gives me peace.**

DAY 9

God is with you on this journey. He isn't distant. He wants to comfort and guide you (Psalms 23:4).

Psalms 23:1 – "The Lord is my shepherd; I have all that I need."

A shepherd guides, protects, and provides for his flock. This is what God wants to do for you. You have to lower your guard and open up to him.

Prayer: Lord, I pray that I would open my heart and let you in totally. Even when I don't feel you next to me, I believe you are there. Thank you for this comfort. I ask that your goodness and mercy follow me all the days of my life.

Today's Proclamation: **I am not alone. God is with me.**

"LET YOUR ROOTS GROW DOWN INTO HIM, AND LET YOUR LIVES BE BUILT ON HIM. THEN YOUR FAITH WILL GROW STRONG IN THE TRUTH YOU WERE TAUGHT, AND YOU WILL OVERFLOW WITH THANKFULNESS."

Colossians 2:7

DAY 10

Psalms 27:8 – "My heart has heard you say, 'Come and talk with me.' And my heart responds, 'Lord, I am coming.'"

You can be confident that you can confide in and lean on God. The Lord will help and teach you (Psalms 27:3-11). He wants you to spend time with him in prayer.

Prayer: Lord, I'm here responding to your call. Please talk to me and show me your way. Teach me how you want me to handle situations and decisions.

Today's Proclamation: **I am firmly rooted in Christ and built up in him.**

DAY 11

There is a season when the seed *grows*. It goes from being planted to flowering and producing fruit. When a seed is in the ground, it is hard to imagine what exactly that tree and fruit will look like in the future. You go through similar seasons where you aren't sure the seed will ever grow big enough to produce anything. With God, the good seed will continue to grow (Psalms 1:3).

Prayer: Lord, make me to be like a Palm tree planted by the water and strong like a Cedar that I would produce fruit in my season and my leaf will not wither. Thank you for the good seeds that have been planted in my life and that I have planted. May the seeds continue to grow as your word says.

Today's Proclamation: **I am sowing good seeds and producing Godly fruit.**

DAY 12

Psalms 46:10 - "Be still and know that I am God! I will be exalted among the nations; I will be exalted in the Earth!"

There is a time for action, and there is a time for waiting. There are times we need to stop for a minute and be silent. Try setting an alarm for 2 minutes. Then, say the prayer below, close your eyes, and wait. Let God's peace fill the silence.

Prayer: Lord, I pray that I would be still and know you are God. And, that I would stop putting limits on your love and power. Be exalted through my life.

Today's Proclamation: **I am a believer and not a doubter.**

"SHOW ME THE RIGHT
PATH, O LORD; POINT
OUT THE ROAD FOR ME
TO FOLLOW. LEAD ME
BY YOUR TRUTH AND
TEACH ME, FOR YOU
ARE THE GOD WHO
SAVES ME. ALL DAY
LONG I PUT MY HOPE IN
YOU."

Psalms 25:4-5

DAY 13

Sometimes while you are trying to wait for God's direction, family and friends are asking for details that you don't have. It can cause you to feel embarrassed or stressed for not having a plan or knowing the answers. Stand firm on Psalms 25:3 that says you can let go of those emotions. It's okay to wait.

Prayer: Lord, don't let me give into feelings of embarrassment or the need to rush. I pray that you will help me stand firm on your word – Psalms 25:5, knowing that while I wait you will teach and lead me.

Today's Proclamation: **I am given strength in exchange for weakness.**

DAY 14

You've completed two weeks! Each day you are getting stronger and keeping God's word close to your heart. Be encouraged and know that your persistence will pay off.

> *Matthew 7:7-8 – "Keep on asking, and you will receive what you ask for. Keep on seeking, and you will find. Keep on knocking, and the door will be opened to you. For everyone who asks, receives. Everyone who seeks, finds. And to everyone who knocks, the door will be opened."*

What an amazing promise!

Prayer: Lord, thank you for your Word for it states in Luke 1:37 that "the word of God will never fail." So, I am seeking your will in my life. I'm asking for [insert your need here]. I thank you that when I ask, it prompts you to act.

Today's Proclamation: **I have a spirit of power, love and a sound mind.**

DAY 15

"It is good to give thanks to the Lord, to sing praises to the Most High." - Psalms 92:1

It doesn't matter if you have a good singing voice or not. God loves to hear you sing and give thanks. Where you are doesn't matter either! You can do it in the car on the way to work or in the shower. Even when you are going through a rough time, there is power in giving thanks for the victory that you can't see yet. Just shout it out!

Prayer: Lord, I thank you. Thank you that I woke up this morning. Thank you for this chance to talk to you. I pray that you would put a song in my heart today as a reminder to sing praises to you.

Today's Proclamation: **I declare the lovingkindness of God in my life.**

Day 16

Did you know that "it is impossible to please God without faith?" – Hebrews 11:6. When you are in a time of waiting and seeking, it can seem like nothing is happening. Maybe you've been reading this devotional every day, but you aren't noticing a change yet.

> Hebrews 11:1 - "Faith shows the reality of what we hope for; it is the evidence of things we cannot see."

Prayer: Lord, I believe you exist, and I pray that you would give me a new perspective today. I pray my faith would be built up like that of Abel's – acceptable in your sight. Thank you for helping my unbelief.

Today's Proclamation: **I have faith.**

"INTELLIGENT PEOPLE
ARE ALWAYS READY TO
LEARN. THEIR EARS ARE
OPEN FOR KNOWLEDGE."

Proverbs 18:15

DAY 17

Psalms 119:29 – "Keep me from lying to myself; give me the privilege of knowing your instructions."

Faith doesn't mean ignoring or not facing a situation. Psalms 119:29 is clear about seeking God to help you not lie to yourself. It is when the honesty comes in that you will know God's instructions. Acknowledge whatever is going on and seek clarity. Spend a few minutes in silence after you pray, and let God respond.

Prayer: Lord, is there something that I'm not seeing clearly about? I pray you would open my eyes and my heart to the truth. And through this truth, you would help me hear your instructions on how to handle or react to it.

Today's Proclamation: **My ears are open to the Lord.**

"SHOW ME THE RIGHT PATH, O LORD; POINT OUT THE ROAD FOR ME TO FOLLOW."

Psalms 25:4

Day 18

It takes faith to pray. So, instead of being quick to act and slow to pray, be *quick to pray*. Prayer is about aligning your heart's preferences with God's will. Then, your activity is directed by God.

> "Seek his will in all you do, and he will show you which path to take." – Proverbs 3:6

Prayer: Lord, thank you for caring about which path I take. I pray that my heart and mind would be aligned with your will. Help me remember your scriptures and to hear your voice throughout the day.

Today's Proclamation: **I am slow to speak, quick to hear, and slow to anger.**

DAY 19

It also takes faith to stay calm when you really want to run around the house or office freaking out. Ever plan on something and it did not go as planned? What about run late for an appointment or meeting even though you put forth the effort to get there early? During moments like these, you can proclaim Exodus 14:14 – "The Lord himself will fight for you. Just stay calm." Or, Deuteronomy 31:8 – "Do not be afraid or discouraged, for the Lord will personally go ahead of you. He will be with you; he will neither fail you nor abandon you."

> *Whatever is out of your control, is still in God's control.*

Prayer: Lord, you know there are moments where I'm anxious or having trouble staying calm. I pray you'd help me remember Exodus and Deuteronomy, so I will stop and claim your peace.

Today's Proclamation: **I believe God is fighting for me.**

DAY 20

2 Corinthians 1:4 states that "He comforts us in all our troubles so that we can comfort others. When they are troubled, we will be able to give them the same comfort God has given us."

Life isn't all rainbows and roses. You face real problems. Have you ever talked to someone facing a similar circumstance? There is a level of reassurance knowing that you aren't the only one and learning from their experience. God wants to use you as a comfort to others as well.

Prayer: Lord, comfort me as I face the challenges ahead today. I know that your comfort doesn't mean that everything is going to be exactly the way I want it to be. I do ask that you give me strength and help me to see your hand in my life. Show me how what I am going through can be used to help someone else. Put a desire in me to be willing to step out in faith and support others.

Today's Proclamation: **I am called by God.**

"THIS IS REAL LOVE—NOT
THAT WE LOVED GOD,
BUT THAT HE LOVED US
AND SENT HIS SON AS A
SACRIFICE TO TAKE
AWAY OUR SINS."

1 John 4:10

DAY 21

You've hit your 21st day! Congratulations on keeping up your daily 5-minute routine. Even if you've missed a day or two, keep pushing forward. A reminder to do just that is:

> *Philippians 3:13 "No, dear brothers and sisters, I have not achieved it, but I focus on this one thing: Forgetting the past and looking forward to what lies ahead."*

Why was Paul determined to push ahead? Because he had experienced the goodness of the Lord, and he knew God was in control of the future. Have you experienced something and without a doubt knew you just had to feel / do that again?

Prayer: Lord, I want to experience your goodness and presence in my life in a way that I never have. Let the experience build a passion inside of me to pursue you with the determination of Paul.

Today's Proclamation: **I am deeply loved by God.**

DAY 22

Ephesians 1:19-20 "I also pray that you will understand the incredible greatness of God's power for us who believe in him. This is the same mighty power that raised Christ from the dead and seated him on the place of honor at God's right hand in the heavenly realms."

It can be hard to grasp the power and greatness because it's so tremendous! You don't have to downplay it. Or rationalize it. You can be in awe. You have access to this power because you are a child of God. Let yourself be excited.

Prayer: Lord, even the thought of your power amazes me. It's hard to imagine it with my mind; yet, I believe. Continue to do a work in my heart to build my unbelief and help me to tap into your greatness.

Today's Proclamation: I am the head and not the tail; above and not beneath.

"IT IS GOOD TO
PROCLAIM YOUR
UNFAILING LOVE IN THE
MORNING, YOUR
FAITHFULNESS IN THE
EVENING."

Psalms 92:2

DAY 23

Every day is a new day, and this is a new morning. Did you know that each day God's mercies are renewed?

> *Lamentations 3:23 - "Great is his faithfulness; his mercies begin afresh each morning."*

Now, that's amazing! God doesn't hold a grudge about yesterday. He just wants you to admit to him any missteps and for you to start your day with a fresh perspective. Let go of the wrongs, the successes, all of the past. Today is a blank slate. Make it great.

Prayer: Lord, I am so grateful for your faithfulness and mercy. I give you my yesterday. I lay it down at your feet. Guide me today. Give me wisdom in every decision I make and word I say. I praise your holy name. Thank you, Lord.

Today's Proclamation: **I am facing today with a fresh perspective.**

DAY 24

Matthew 11:30 - "For my yoke is easy to bear, and the burden I give you is light."

Do you feel weighed down with responsibility at home or at work? It can be difficult to manage all of it when you are being pulled in so many directions. God's word says that he will carry it for you; sounds amazing, right? It can be easier said than done. You have to be honest about the load you are carrying and unpack it. As you take each piece out and give it to God, it lightens your load. Try it. Think of what needs to be given to God today, and then pray.

Prayer: Lord, I believe your word is true. I am carrying quite a bit around, and I ask that as I speak each thing you would lighten the weight I am carrying. I want to give you [say each responsibility, worry, care, everything that you've got on your mind]. Thank you for carrying all of these for me.

Today's Proclamation: **The Lord is enough! I am letting go and letting God handle it.**

Day 25

God delights in **you**. He rejoices over **you**. **You** are important to God. In case the fact that he delights and rejoices over you isn't enough, he will also calm your fears. By letting God into your life, you are letting in his love. For Zephaniah 3:17 states

> *"...He will take delight in you with gladness. With his love, he will calm all your fears. He will rejoice over you with joyful songs."*

Now, that's a good breakfast.

Prayer: Lord, thank you for being my Lord and savior. I pray your love would penetrate ever part of me and calm all my fears. My fear of embarrassment, failure, not being good enough, [say any fear you have]. Let your songs of rejoicing fill me today.

Today's Proclamation: **I am a delight.**

"TEACH ME HOW TO LIVE, O LORD. LEAD ME ALONG THE RIGHT PATH, FOR MY ENEMIES ARE WAITING FOR ME."

Psalms 27:11

DAY 26

Way to go, you are on Day 26 of God's breakfast! It is through this pursuit of God in your life that produces fruit like joy, peace, and faith (Galatians 5:22-23). For with wisdom and knowledge comes joy (Proverbs 2:10). As you are getting to the end of this devotional. Ask God to continue to teach you how to live (Psalms 27:11).

Prayer: Lord, thank you for today and for your word. I want to continue to write it on my heart. I want to approach each day with a new revelation of who you are. Give me direction on how much time you want me to spend with you each morning, and place in me the deep desire to set aside that time for you.

Today's Proclamation: **I am full of joy!**

"HE SAID [DANIEL],
'PRAISE THE NAME OF
GOD FOREVER AND
EVER, FOR HE HAS ALL
WISDOM
AND POWER.' "

Daniel 2:20

Day 27

Throughout scripture, there are times that God asks a question knowing the answer. It is a teaching method to get you thinking. A way of breaking your thought and bringing a different perspective. This is what is happening in Jeremiah 32:27 – "I am the Lord, the God of all the peoples of the world. Is anything too hard for me?"

He is the Lord of Lords. King of Kings. El Shaddai. God Almighty. He wants you to know that nothing is too hard. *Let that fact sink down inside of your heart.*

Prayer: Lord, there are times that I am full of joy and times that I doubt even though your word says that you are enough. I ask for forgiveness of any unbelief, and I pray you would help me to grab onto the realness of your love, faithfulness, and power.

Today's Proclamation: **I have peace because nothing is too hard for my God.**

DAY 28

Ephesians 2:10 – "For we are God's masterpiece. He has created us anew in Christ Jesus, so we can do the good things he planned for us long ago."

God created you and through salvation, you can now walk out the destiny God has prepared for you. He made a specific plan for you in advance before you were even born. Trust the shepherd to guide, provide, and protect you.

Prayer: Lord, thank you for creating a plan for me and my life. Since your love for me is constant and endless, I ask you, Lord, to finish every good thing that you've begun in me. Help me to feel empowered to walk into the good things you have prepared for me and give me a passion to do what pleases you.

Today's Proclamation: I am a masterpiece.

"COMMIT YOUR ACTIONS TO THE LORD, AND YOUR PLANS WILL SUCCEED."

Proverbs 16:3

Day 29

Jeremiah 29:11 – "For I know the plans I have for you," says the Lord. "They are plans for good and not for disaster, to give you a future and a hope."

God plans for you are good! He wants you to live an abundant life. John 10:10 states that "The thief's purpose is to steal and kill and destroy. My purpose is to give them a rich and satisfying life."

Prayer: Lord, thank you for saving me from the thief's plans. I pray my will and mind would be in alignment with you. And, that all the plans you have for me would come to be just as you've promised.

Today's Proclamation: **I have an abundant life.**

Day 30

Isaiah 55:8-9 – "'My thoughts are nothing like your thoughts,' says the Lord. 'And my ways are far beyond anything you could imagine. For just as the heavens are higher than the earth, so my ways are higher than your ways and my thoughts higher than your thoughts.'"

Thankfully, God's thoughts and plans are so much bigger than ours.

Prayer: Lord, I get frustrated sometimes because I'm thinking things should be working out a specific way. I get an idea and forget that your ways are greater than mine. I want my faith and peace in your timing and process to increase.

Today's Proclamation: **I trust God's plan.**

ACKNOWLEDGMENTS

God truly is good. His never-failing love has gotten me through the toughest, darkest hours and the most exciting, miraculous seasons. Without him, I wouldn't be alive and thriving today. I'm also grateful for the wonderful friends and family that he has blessed me with on this journey. Thank you for all of the encouragement, cheerleading, and support you've given me (you know who you are!).

May God bless and keep you. May his everlasting love and peace rest upon you. And, may you never have to go without breakfast again!

37556045R00040